PUBLIC LIBRARY DISTRICT OF COLUMBIA

D1252076

Green Machines
Eco-friendly Rides

Lynn Peppas

🌳 Crabtree Publishing Company

www.crabtreebooks.com

Created by Bobbie Kalman

Author
Lynn Peppas

Editorial director
Kathy Middleton

Project editor
Paul Challen

Editors
Adrianna Morganelli
Crystal Sikkens

Proofreaders
Rachel Stuckey
Janine Belzak

Photo research
Melissa McClellan

Design
Tibor Choleva

Print coordinator
Katherine Berti

Production coordinator
Margaret Amy Salter

Prepress technicians
Margaret Amy Salter
Ken Wright

Consultant
Rob Booth M.Eng., P.Eng., Applied Environmental Science Ltd

Illustrations
All illustrations by Leif Peng

Photographs
© Tibor Choleva (page 29)
Dreamstime.com: © Dariusz Kopestynski (table of contents page); © Publicimage (page 4); © Gyuszko (page 5 top); © Arenacreative (page 9 top); © Felix Abrudan (page 9 bottom); © Roza (page 10); © Anthony Hall (page 11 bottom); © Svetlana Gatova (page 11 top); © Jim Parkin (pages 12–13); © Brian Sullivan (page 13 top); © Ivan Cholakov (page 15 bottom); © Jiawangkun (page 16 inset); © Folco Banfi (pages 16–17); © Bncc369 (page 19 middle); © Kotowork (page 23 top);© Svetlana Gatova (page 23 bottom); © Radu Razvan Gheorghe (page 28); © Jan Kranendonk (page 31 top)
istockphoto: ImageegamI (page 25 inset)
© John Bear–Pontiac, Buick, GMC, Cadillac (page 12 inset)
© Gordon Lindqvist, adelaide-in-photos.blogspot.com (page 21)
Public Domain: Hax0rw4ng (page 18); Leew (page 24 bottom)
Shutterstock.com: cover; © Maksim Toome (title page); © Vyacheslav Osokin (page 5 bottom); © Roman Sigaev (page 7 top); © think4photop (pages 6–7); © dusko (page 6 bottom); © Fred Leonero (page 7 bottom); © elwynn (page 8); © Carolina K. Smith, M.D. (page 12 bottom inset); © Annavee (page 12 top inset); ©LovelaceMedia (page 14); © Michael Rubin (page 15 top); © John Kropewnicki (page 17 inset); © Jose Gil (page 19 top and bottom); Shi Yali (page 20 bottom); © Eric Broder Van Dyke (page 20 top); © paul prescott (page 22); Monkey Business Images (pages 24–25); © devi (page 24 top); Kobby Dagan (page 26); © Olga Besnard (page 27); © jbor (page 30 top); © Chad McDermott (pages 30–31)

Library and Archives Canada Cataloguing in Publication

Peppas, Lynn
      Green machines : eco-friendly rides / Lynn Peppas.

(Vehicles on the move)
Includes index.
Issued also in electronic format.
ISBN 978-0-7787-2729-3 (bound).--ISBN 978-0-7787-2736-1 (pbk.)

      1. Alternative fuel vehicles--Juvenile literature. 2. Electric vehicles--Juvenile literature. I. Title. II. Series: Vehicles on the move

TL216.5.P46 2011   j629.22'9   C2011-900138-1

Library of Congress Cataloging-in-Publication Data

Peppas, Lynn.
   Green machines : eco-friendly rides / Lynn Peppas.
      p. cm. -- (Vehicles on the move)
   Includes index.
   ISBN 978-0-7787-2736-1 (pbk. : alk. paper) -- ISBN 978-0-7787-2729-3 (reinforced library binding : alk. paper) -- ISBN 978-1-4271-9698-9 (electronic (pdf))
   1. Alternative fuel vehicles--Juvenile literature. 2. Motor vehicles--Technological innovations--Juvenile literature. 3. Green technology--Juvenile literature. I. Title.
   TL216.5.P47 2011
   629.2--dc22

                                                   2010052346

Crabtree Publishing Company

www.crabtreebooks.com   1-800-387-7650

Printed in the U.S.A./022011/CJ20101228

Copyright © **2011 CRABTREE PUBLISHING COMPANY.** All rights reserved. No part of this publication may be reproduced, stored in a retrieval system or be transmitted in any form or by any means, electronic, mechanical, photocopying, recording, or otherwise, without the prior written permission of Crabtree Publishing Company. In Canada: We acknowledge the financial support of the Government of Canada through the Canada Book Fund for our publishing activities.

Published in Canada
Crabtree Publishing
616 Welland Ave.
St. Catharines, ON
L2M 5V6

Published in the United States
Crabtree Publishing
PMB 59051
350 Fifth Avenue, 59th Floor
New York, New York 10118

Published in the United Kingdom
Crabtree Publishing
Maritime House
Basin Road North, Hove
BN41 1WR

Published in Australia
Crabtree Publishing
386 Mt. Alexander Rd.
Ascot Vale (Melbourne)
VIC 3032

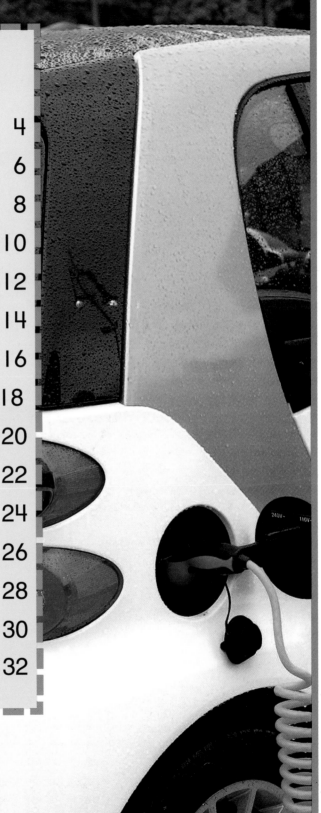

Contents

Green vehicles

Green vehicles are good for Earth. Vehicles are machines that carry people and things to different places. Green vehicles are not always green in color. They come in many different colors. They are called "green" because they are better for the environment than ordinary vehicles. Some go farther on less fuel. Others use fuel that does not pollute the air.

This public transportation bus is powered by natural gas. It pollutes the air much less than an ordinary bus.

Good for the planet

Green vehicles come in all shapes and sizes. They do many different jobs. Vehicles such as trucks, buses, and cars can be green. Green vehicles drive cleaner and are less harmful to Earth.

Electric vehicles run on electrical power only. They do not create any pollution.

Some vehicles are green because they don't use any fuel at all. Bicycles and roller blades use human power. They don't create pollution, and they help keep us healthy.

Fuel makes them go

Every vehicle needs fuel to make it move. Many vehicles use **fossil fuels**. Fossil fuels such as coal and oil are taken from deep inside Earth. They are nonrenewable. This means that Earth cannot make more when they are gone.

Oil rigs remove crude oil from deep inside Earth.

Crude oil is turned into gasoline in oil refineries.

An endless supply

Some green vehicles use fossil fuels but they travel farther on them. Some use electricity. Others use fuel made from plants. These are renewable. Renewable fuels do not run out. Earth can make more.

Corn can be used to make fuel for vehicles.

Global warming

Earth's climate is getting hotter. This is called **global warming**. People, animals, and crops are affected by global warming. Some scientists believe that global warming is caused by pollution. Vehicles that burn fossil fuels pollute the air.

Air-friendly

Green vehicles make less pollution when they travel. They pollute less because they use less fossil fuels. Sometimes they do not pollute at all when they use other types of fuels. Green vehicles are less harmful to Earth.

Driving small cars and riding bicycles when possible reduces pollution.

More and more people are buying smaller, Earth-friendly cars. They use less fossil fuels to travel the same distance as other cars.

Microcars

Microcars are very small vehicles on four wheels. Micro means very small. Microcars carry only two people. Most microcars have gasoline-powered engines. They can travel a long way on one tank of gas. This means less pollution.

There are many different kinds of microcars. This one has a removable roof.

City driving

Vehicles use more fuel in the city than they do on the highway. Microcars are good vehicles for making trips around town. They do not need a lot of space for parking. Microcars can fit easily into small parking spaces.

Police officers drive microcars in some cities where streets are narrow.

Microcars are very practical when parking in large, crowded cities.

Flexible fuel vehicles

A flexible fuel vehicle has one engine that can run on two different kinds of fuel. **Flexible** means that something can easily change. Flexible fuel vehicles can change what kind of fuel they run on. Sometimes they are called flex-fuel vehicles.

flex-fuel truck

Veggie power!

Most flex-fuel vehicles run on gasoline. Their engines can also use fuels such as ethanol or a mixture of gasoline and ethanol. Ethanol fuel is made from plants such as corn or potatoes. They are renewable because farmers can grow more.

potatoes

Ethanol fuel is produced at refinery plants such as the one shown here.

Hybrid vehicles

A **hybrid** is something that is made from two different things. A hybrid vehicle uses two different motors to make it move. Each motor needs a different kind of fuel. One motor runs on gasoline. The other motor runs on an electric battery.

Many American car companies make hybrid vehicles such as this Ford Fusion.

Switched on!

Hybrid vehicles run on the greener, cleaner fuel when they can. When electricity is not available, hybrid vehicles use their gas-powered motors. They use less gasoline and make less pollution.

Some cities use hybrid buses for public transportation.

engine

power control unit

electricity

generator

motor

power split device

Hybrid vehicles have two motors: an ordinary fossil fuel engine and an electric motor.

Electric vehicles

An electric vehicle is sometimes called an E-vehicle. E stands for electric. An E-vehicle runs on electrical power only. E-vehicles usually have more than one motor. They store power in large batteries. The batteries in the car fuel the motors.

One of the best things about E-vehicles is that they do not produce pollution.

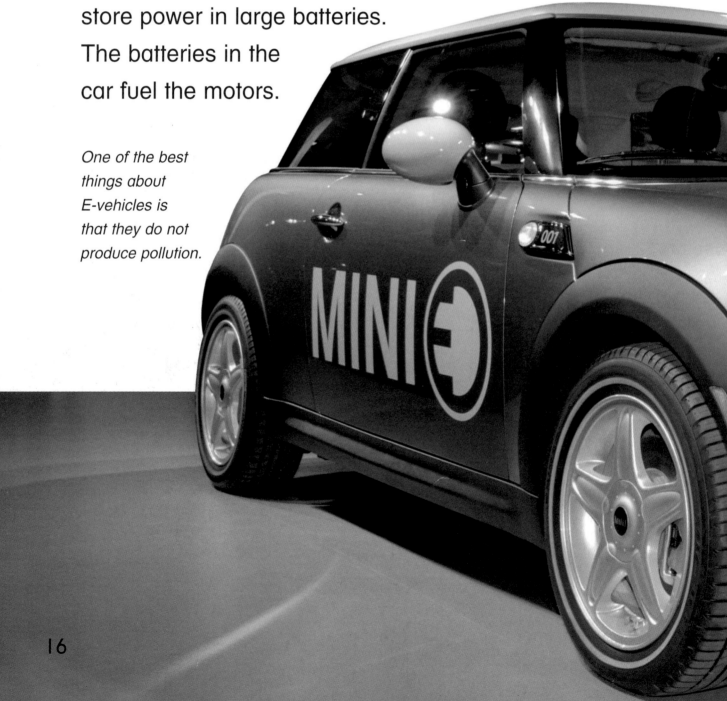

Charging up

Batteries are recharged, or fueled, by plugging them into an electrical outlet. They can fuel up from home or at a charging station. Charging stations are a lot like gasoline stations. But an E-vehicle is "filled up" with electricity instead of gasoline. It takes more time to fill up on electricity.

Charging stations for E-vehicles are marked with a sign that looks like an electric plug.

ELECTRIC VEHICLE CHARGING STATION

MINI E

Hydrogen fuel-cell vehicles

Some E-vehicles draw their power from a fuel cell instead of a battery. A **fuel cell** turns a chemical called **hydrogen** into electricity. The vehicle runs on the electric power created by the cell.

This bus from Perth, Western Australia, runs on a hydrogen fuel cell.

The silent type

Vehicles that run on electricity do not produce any air pollution. They do not make noise pollution either. It is hard to hear an E-vehicle driving down the road because it runs very quietly.

Fuel cells were used for the first time in 1965-1966. The U.S. space agency NASA used them to power its Gemini spacecraft.

Big cars and trucks can run on fuel cell power like this custom-built, hydrogen fuel-cell powered Hummer H2.

Solar vehicles

Solar means "of the Sun." A **solar vehicle** has an electric motor that is powered by fuel from the Sun. The Sun shines on solar panels. These panels change the Sun's energy into electricity. Electricity powers the motor.

solar panels

Racing solar cars are powered by the Sun. They get electricity from solar panels on the top of the cars.

Fun for the Sun

Some solar vehicles carry solar panels on top of them. Most people cannot buy this type of vehicle yet. However, some people collect the Sun's energy from solar panels on their homes in a battery. Then they use the battery to power their vehicle.

The Australian Tindo is the world's first solar-powered bus.

Tri-cars

A **tri-car** has three wheels instead of four. Tri means three. Some tri-cars have two wheels in the front, and one in the back. Others have one wheel in the front and two in the back.

Three-wheeler delivery vehicles, like this one, are very common in India.

Small but mighty

Tri-cars are small cars that can seat one or two people only. Some have engines that use gasoline for fuel. They are lightweight, however, so they can travel farther on a tank of gas. Some tri-cars are even greener because they have electric motors.

This is an air-powered tri-car. It uses compressed air to run its engines.

This tri-car is used by the New York City Police Department.

Green bicycles

All bicycles are green vehicles. They have two wheels that move in a single line. They move with human power and do not make any pollution. Bicycles are quiet. They are also a healthy way to travel to school, work, or on a short trip.

A bike taxi is a covered bike with three wheels used to drive people around in large cities.

A velomobile is a covered bicycle. It looks like a little car. A velomobile has pedals like a bicycle. Some have two or three wheels. They carry just one person.

Working bicycles

People ride bicycles at work, too. Police officers ride bicycles to patrol communities. Bike couriers deliver letters and small parcels quickly in crowded cities. Their bikes get them through traffic jams easily. And there is no need to worry about finding a good parking space!

Electric bicycles

Electric bicycles are sometimes called E-bikes. They look like a bicycle. They are powered by both human power and an electric motor. E-bikes have rechargeable batteries. The electric motor draws power from the batteries.

People in China use electric bikes to get around cities every day. China has about 25 million cars on the road and four times as many E-bikes.

This is a modern E-bike on display.

Starting up

E-bikes travel different speeds depending on the size of their motors. Some can travel up to 20 miles per hour (32 km/h). On some E-bikes, the rider must pedal to start the motor. On others, the motor can be started by a control on the handlebars.

Scooters and mopeds

Scooters are small motorcycles with a floorboard for the driver's feet. Scooters do not have pedals. Many run on fuel such as gasoline. They are green vehicles because they travel farther on a tank of gas than a car or truck. Some scooters run on electric motors. They are greener because they do not produce any air pollution.

Scooters have smaller wheels than a regular motorcycle.

Bike look-alike

Some small motorcycles are called **mopeds**. The name comes from combining letters from the two words *motor* and *pedal*. Put them together and you get *moped*. Most mopeds look more like a bicycle than a motorcycle or scooter. A moped has a pedal that starts its engine.

Mopeds are great for city driving. They can travel up to speeds of 30 mph (48 km/h).

Segway PTs

A Segway PT is a one-passenger vehicle. PT stands for personal transporter, which means it can move one person. A rider must stand up while driving a Segway PT. The Segway PT has a floorboard between two wheels that are side by side. Riders lean on the handlebars in the direction they want to travel.

Segways are used on golf courses, too.

Gliding along

A Segway PT glides forward very quietly. This is because each wheel is operated by an electric motor. The motors are powered by rechargeable batteries. Police officers and theme park workers often use them to safely move through crowds of people.

Taking a tour on a Segway is always fun! A Segway can travel at speeds of up to 12.5 mph (20 km/h).

Words to know and Index

electric bicycles
pages 26–27

green vehicles
pages 4–5, 7, 9

microcars
pages 10–11

scooters
page 28–29

tri-cars
pages 22–23

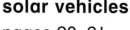

solar vehicles
pages 20–21